Island Footprints

Jillian Powell

Editorial consultants:
Cliff Moon and Lorraine Petersen

nasen
NASEN House, 4/5 Amber Business Village, Amber Close,
Amington, Tamworth, Staffordshire B77 4RP

Rising Stars UK Ltd.
22 Grafton Street, London W1S 4EX
www.risingstars-uk.com

Published 2007
Reprinted 2008 (twice)

Cover design: Button plc
Illustrator: Aleksandar Sotirovski
Text design and typesetting: Andy Wilson
Publisher: Gill Budgell
Commissioning editor: Catherine Baker
Publishing manager: Lesley Densham
Editor: Clare Robertson
Editorial consultants: Cliff Moon and Lorraine Petersen

British Library Cataloguing in Publication Data.
A CIP record for this book is available from the British Library

ISBN: 978-1-84680-210-2

Printed by Craft Print International Limited, Singapore

Contents

Characters 4

Scene 1: **Shipwrecked** 7

Scene 2: **Footprints in the sand** 17

Scene 3: **The trap** 29

Scene 4: **Stuck in a hole** 37

Drama ideas 47

Characters

Dan Gore He's smart, but can he outwit Callum Watts?

Eddie Dan's best friend.

Kim Classmate of Eddie and Dan.

Callum Watts
The class bully.

Liam Callum's dopey sidekick.

Narrator The narrator tells the story.

Scene 1

Shipwrecked

Narrator Dan wakes up. He is on a white beach.
His ship has been in a bad storm.
He is shipwrecked.
But where are the rest of his class?

Dan Hello? Is there anyone there? Hello?

Eddie Helloooooo!

Dan Who's that?

Eddie It's me, Eddie.

Dan Eddie. Am I glad to see you!

Eddie Me too, mate.

Dan What happened?

Eddie Our ship got into trouble – remember?
There were these massive waves.

Dan Oh, yes! I remember.
There was a bang.
Everything went dark.
We had to bail out.

Eddie So we're … shipwrecked.
But where are the others?
We can't be the only ones here.
Try shouting together.

Dan and Eddie Hello! Hello!

Narrator Then Dan and Eddie hear something.

Kim Help!

Dan Wait a minute.
That sounds like Kim.

Eddie Over here!

Kim Thank goodness!
I just woke up and I was alone.
I was really scared.

Dan Me too.

Kim How did we get here?

Eddie In that, I guess.

Narrator Eddie points to a rubber boat
on the beach.

Kim Hey, we've got a boat.

Dan I don't think so.
Look, it's bust!

Narrator Dan kicks the boat.
A rock has made a hole in it.

Kim What do we do now?

Eddie Well, I don't know about you,
but I'm hungry.

Kim And thirsty.

Dan Has anyone got anything to eat?

Eddie I've got this bit of chocolate.
It's a bit wet, but we can eat that.

Dan Hey guys, look what I've got.

Narrator Dan pulls out a torch.

Eddie Wicked! Just what we'll need
when it gets dark.

Dan My dad got it for me.
I knew it would come in handy one day.

Kim We need to find some food and water.

Eddie There's nothing over that way.
I've been looking.

Kim Let's try over here.

Narrator Suddenly, Dan freezes.

Dan Oh no!

Kim What's up?

Dan Just look what the waves threw up!

Eddie I don't believe it. Callum Watts,
of all people.

Kim And his sidekick, Liam.

Eddie That's just great.
Shipwrecked with a meathead
and a loser!

Kim Well, we're all in this together.
He has to be friends with us now.

Dan I wouldn't bank on it.
Look at his face.

Narrator Callum and Liam come towards them.

Callum They say a lot of rubbish
gets washed up on beaches.

Liam And we've just found it.

Dan Hey, Callum, Liam.
Have you found any water yet?

Callum Are you talking to me, Gore?

Dan Well … it looks like it's just us, Callum.
We'd better try and get along.

Callum You reckon?

Eddie Well, it's a bit stupid
to be enemies here isn't it?

Callum Is it?

Kim Look, what's the point of fighting,
Callum?

Callum Who asked you?

Dan Don't pick on her.
She's hungry and thirsty.
We all are.

Kim We just want to know
if you've found any water yet.

Liam Like we'd tell you.

Dan You can't be serious!

Callum Remember being a grass?
Getting me into trouble with Hawkins?

Dan So you want to carry on the fight?
We're in the middle of nowhere.
We're stuck on this island, and you
want to fight. Smart, Watts.

Callum Um … where do you think
you're going?

Eddie We need to find water,
and something to eat.

Callum Well, not over here you don't.
This is our bit of the island, okay?

Kim Don't be stupid.
It's no one's island.
We're all in the same …

Liam Boat? She's sharp, isn't she?

Dan We're not trying to pick a fight.
We just want to get some food
and water.

Callum Yeah, well you can do that
on *your* bit of the island.

Dan You really are being a pratt, Watts.

Callum Big mistake, calling me names.
What's this you've got?

Narrator Callum grabs Dan's torch.

Callum This will come in handy, thanks.

Dan Give that back, it's mine!

Callum Not now it isn't.

Liam Don't mess with the big boys, Gore. You'll never win.

Callum See this? I am going to draw a line in the sand. We stay this side, you stay that side. Got it?

Kim You're mad.

Callum Cross this line, and you'll see what I *am* like when I'm mad.

Dan Come on guys, he's not worth it.

Scene 2

Footprints in the sand

Eddie I can't believe how stupid Callum is being.

Dan I can't believe he took my torch. We needed that.

Kim Hey, guys! Look over here.

Dan What is it?

Eddie Footprints!

Dan You know what this means …

Kim There must be someone else on the island.

Dan Better follow them. Come on!

Narrator They follow the footprints. The prints lead into the jungle. Suddenly, they hear the splash of water. It is a waterfall.

Eddie Result! Man, I am so thirsty. I could drink forever!

Dan Me too!

Kim It's lovely and cold!

Narrator They all have a long drink. Then they start splashing about in the water.

Dan This is great. Good job you saw those footprints, Kim.

Kim I was just thinking, they are huge aren't they? I mean, look at our footprints next to them.

Eddie They are a bit big.

Dan You're right. They're massive.

Kim Bigger than a man's, right?

Eddie Even a man with big feet!

Kim I wonder who – or what – has footprints this big …

Narrator Kim bends down to look closer.
Just then, something huge comes
out of the jungle behind her.
It is very big. It is very hairy.
It looks like King Kong in the movie.
Dan and Eddie freeze.

Dan Um … Kim …

Eddie Kim, you might want to …

Narrator But it is too late.
The giant gorilla grabs Kim.
She screams. It turns and
takes her off into the jungle.

Dan Eddie, it's got Kim!

Eddie I … I think I'm going to faint!

Dan You can't. We have to save Kim.

Eddie Did you see its eyes?

Dan Did you see its teeth?

Eddie Do gorillas eat meat?

Dan Something tells me this one might!
We have to rescue Kim.

Eddie What shall we do?

Dan I think we should tell the others.
They need to know
what's on this island.
And we may need their help.

Eddie That means going over
his stupid line.

Dan We can't worry about that!
Kim's in danger.
Hurry up, Eddie.
We have to find them, and fast.

Narrator The boys run off through the jungle.
They have to find Callum and Liam
and get them to help.

Dan There they are! Callum! Liam!

Callum Not you again, Gore.
I thought I told you ...

Liam We're making a fire. Get lost.

Dan Listen! Kim is in danger.
In fact, we all are.

Eddie There is this thing.
It's like a gorilla,
only much, much bigger.
A sort of monster gorilla.

Narrator Callum and Liam start laughing.

Callum You'll have to do better
than that, you losers.

Dan No, really. I know it sounds mad.
But we saw it.
Large as life … well, larger.
I mean, it was …
bigger than that tree!
And it took Kim.

Eddie There may be others.
There may be loads of them.

Callum Ooh, look. I'm trembling!

Liam Me too …
I've come over all faint!

Dan Stop messing about.
This is serious!

Callum You pair of geeks.
Monster gorillas …
You've been playing too
many computer games.

Narrator Then Dan has an idea.

Dan Look, we can prove it.
Just come and see its footprints.

Eddie Yeah. Just come and look.
Once you've seen the size
of these footprints,
you'll *have* to believe us.

Callum What do you think, Liam?
Shall we go and see
these monster prints?

Liam Ooh … I don't know.
King Kong might get us!

Dan You have to come, Callum.
You both have to come
and see this.

Callum Go on then.
Show us your monster tracks.

Narrator Dan and Eddie lead the others across the sand. They have to find the footprints again.
They have to save Kim.

Scene 3

The trap

Narrator Dan and Eddie show the others the footprints. For a minute, Callum and Liam are quiet.

Eddie Now do you believe us?

Callum Okay, so there is some sort of …
gorilla thing on the island.
What do you want us
to do about it?

Dan You have to help us rescue Kim.

Callum You will owe us for this, Gore.

Liam Big time.

Dan Whatever.

Eddie Now can we start looking for Kim?

Dan Why don't we split up?
We'll cover more ground that way.

Liam And if we find her?

Dan Shout! We may need the four of us
against this brute!

Narrator The boys split up. Dan and Eddie
go back to the waterfall.
Then they follow the tracks
from there.

Dan and Eddie Kim! Kim! Where are you?

Dan You know what, this is stupid!
It might come after us.
We should set some sort of trap.

Eddie I know how to do this.
I've seen it on TV.
We dig a hole and cover it
with leaves and stuff.

Narrator Dan and Eddie find some rocks
and begin to dig a hole.

Dan Keep digging!
It needs to be quite a big hole.

Eddie This is hard work!

Dan Just think of Kim.
She must be so scared!

Narrator Callum and Liam are in
another part of the jungle.

Liam Those footprints sure were big!

Callum If we're lucky, the stupid girl
will just turn up. We'll tell them
we saw off the gorilla.
Then they'll owe us!

Liam Good idea!

Narrator Just then, they hear something.
It sounds like someone singing.

Callum What was that?

Liam It came from behind that rock.

Callum Better take a look.
Hand me that stick.

Narrator Callum and Liam get closer.
They look over the rock.
They can see Kim.
She is alone, singing to herself.
There is a pile of fruit beside her.

Callum (*whispering*) It's not there.
She's on her own.

Liam (*whispering*) Look at all that fruit!
I'm starving!

Narrator Callum and Liam come out from behind the rock.

Callum So where is this monster?
Gore said a giant gorilla
had got you!

Kim Callum, Liam!
Are the others with you?

Liam Never mind them!
Where did you get all this fruit?

Callum And where is this gorilla?
Or were they making it up?
They said you were in danger.

Kim Oh, there's a gorilla all right.
And it's massive …
taller than that tree.
But we're not in danger.
It's kind. It wants to help us.
Look, it brought me all this fruit.
It's lush!

Callum Give us some, then.

Kim I think it's gone to find more.
We can share this with Dan and Eddie.

Callum I don't think so.
They led us on a wild goose chase.
No, we're taking this, thanks.

Narrator Callum and Liam begin
grabbing the fruit.

Kim Hey! Stop it!
That's not fair.
It's for all of us.

Liam Finders keepers.

Callum Get your hairy friend
to find you some more!
See you!

Narrator Callum and Liam make off
with the fruit.

Kim I don't believe you, Callum Watts!

Narrator Kim goes to find the others.

Kim Dan! Eddie! Where are you?

Narrator Dan and Eddie have finished making the trap. They are looking for Kim. Dan sees her first.

Dan Kim! There you are!
We've been so worried.

Eddie Did that monster hurt you?

Kim It's not the gorilla that's a monster.
Just wait till you hear this …

Scene 4

Stuck in a hole

Narrator Kim, Dan and Eddie set out to find Callum and Liam.

Kim There they are!
Look, through the trees!

Dan They didn't get very far.

Eddie Too busy eating all that fruit.

Dan Hey, you two! Come and face us.

Callum What's your problem, Gore?

Dan You're our problem, stealing that food!
The gorilla gave that to Kim.

Kim It was for all of us.

Liam We didn't see any gorilla.

Callum There *was* no gorilla.
You made it up.
You were keeping that food
for yourselves.

Kim Look, I should know.
It carried me off. I was terrified.
But it didn't want to hurt me.
It was helping us, all of us.

Eddie You're a thief, Watts!
And you too, Liam.
You are selfish and greedy and …

Callum What did you call me, you little squirt?

Eddie I said you're a thief!

Callum Right! You'll pay for that!

Kim Stop it! Stop fighting!
This is so stupid.

Narrator But Callum and Liam are ready to fight. They begin walking towards the others. They are getting closer and closer to the gorilla trap.

Eddie Come on then, Watts,
if you want a fight!

Kim Please stop it!

Narrator Dan looks at Eddie.
If they can just get them
to come one more step …

Dan Don't worry, Kim.
They're all talk.

Callum Right, Gore. You've had it!
… Aaaaargh!

Liam What the … Aaaaargh!

Narrator Callum and Liam fall into the trap.
Kim looks shocked.
Then she sees the others laughing.

Kim Did you know that hole was there?

Dan (*laughing*) Yes, we dug it!
It was for the gorilla.

Eddie But it will do for them too!

Callum and Liam Get us out of here!
Help, you morons!

Narrator Dan, Eddie and Kim look down into the hole.

Dan I don't think so, Watts.
I quite like seeing you in a hole!

Callum Okay, you've had your joke.
Now get us out of here!

Eddie I don't think I heard 'please' –
did you, Dan?

Narrator Dan and Eddie are having fun.
But Kim has spotted the gorilla.
It seems to want them to follow it.

Kim Hey, guys, look. I think it's trying to tell us something.

Eddie It's heading for the beach, look.

Kim I think I know why!
Look through the trees.
I think I can see a ship out there.

Eddie Rescue! We're going to be rescued!

Dan We have to get down there – and fast!
It's our only chance.

Eddie What about these two jokers?

Kim We can't leave them here.

Dan No. You're right.
Okay, you idiots.
Your luck is in.
Give us your hands.

Kim Hurry up!
We've got no time to waste!

Narrator Dan and Eddie try to pull the others out. But it is a deep hole. It is hard work.

Kim Hey, look, guys! The gorilla wants to help.

Eddie Stand back, Dan. I want to see their faces.

Narrator Callum and Liam look up in horror. The giant gorilla bends over the hole. Then it reaches down and pulls them out.

Dan Now do you believe us, Watts?

Eddie I wish I had a camera!

Callum Okay, okay. Look, are you sure it's friendly?

Liam It's … It's massive.

Dan Never mind that!
We must get down to the beach.
There is a ship out there.
If we miss it, we might be stuck here forever!

Kim Come on guys, run!

Narrator They all run to the beach.
They jump up and down and wave.
The ship comes closer.
They have been seen.

Kim Oh, look. The gorilla is going back into the jungle.
We didn't even say thank you!

Dan It knew it was our friend, Kim.

Callum Look, Gore.
You'd better have this back.

Narrator Callum gives Dan his torch back.

Dan Okay, thanks.

Narrator Dan smiles at Eddie and Kim.
Somehow he knows
that from now on,
things will be different.

Drama ideas

1

After Scene 1

- With a partner, be Callum and Dan.
- Each explain what you are thinking about the other one at the end of Scene 1. What does Dan want Callum to do, and what does Callum want Dan to do?

After Scene 2

- With your group, discuss what you think will happen next. Will the characters meet the gorilla? Will they rescue Kim?
- Act out your ideas.

2

After Scene 3

- Hotseating: choose one person to be Liam.
- Everyone else can ask Liam questions to find out why he goes along with Callum. Does he like Callum? Does he think Callum is right?

After Scene 4

- Choose a character from the play.
- Take turns to explain to the rest of the group what happens to your character after the play is over.

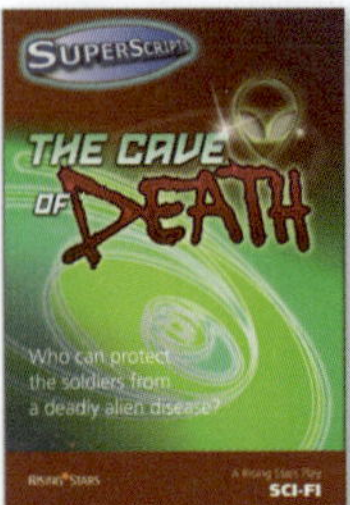

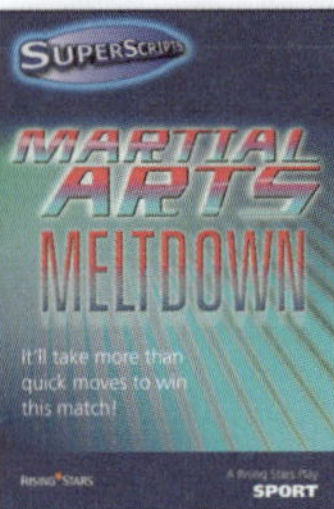

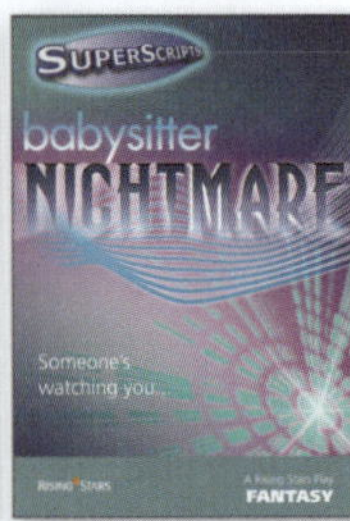

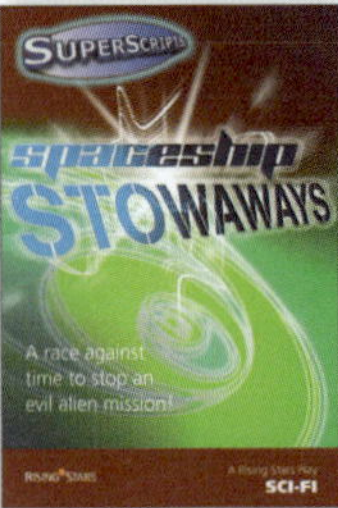

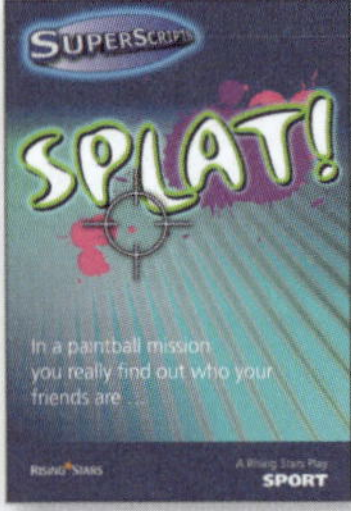

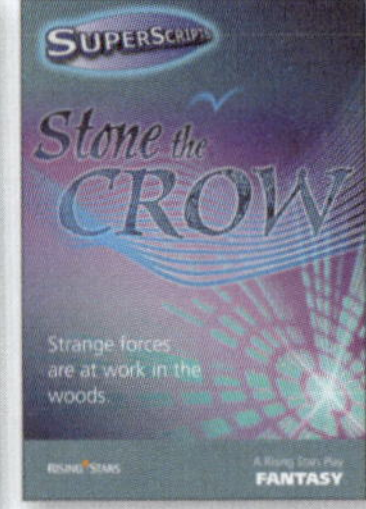

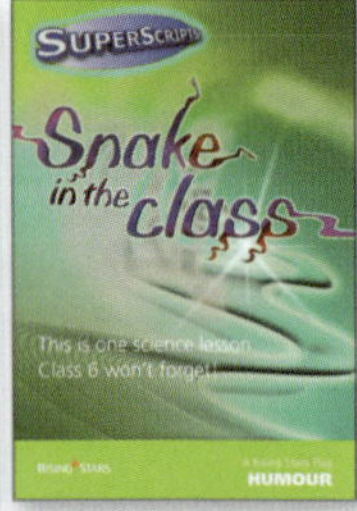

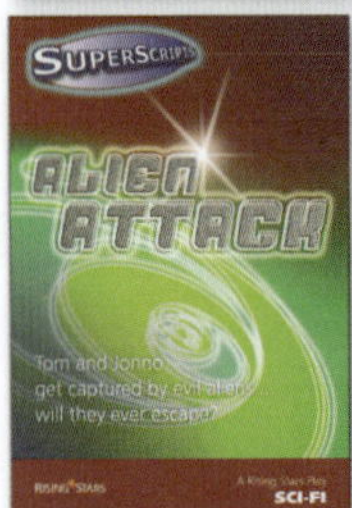

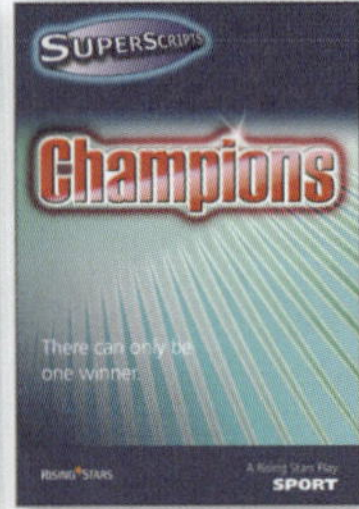

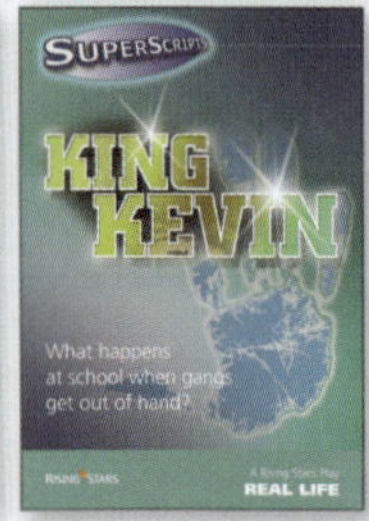

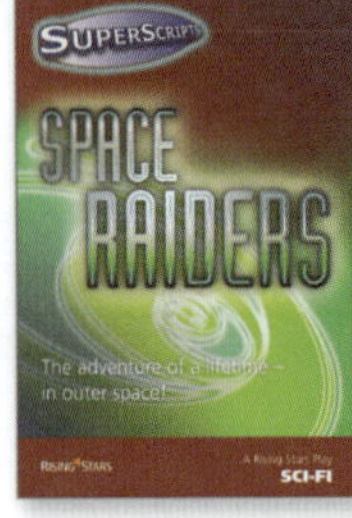

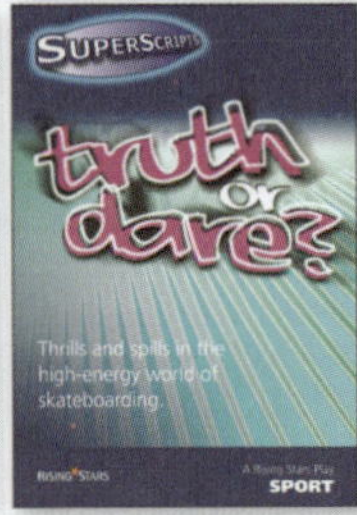

PHONE

0871 47 23 010

www.risingstars-uk.com